THE LOVING GAME

Also by Vernon Scannell

A Mortal Pitch (1957)

Masks of Love (1960)
(*Heinneman Award for Literature, 1960*)

A Sense of Danger (1962)
(*Recommended by the Poetry Book Society*)

Walking Wounded (1965)

Epithets of War (1969)

Selected Poems (1971)

The Winter Man (1973)

THE LOVING GAME

Poems by

VERNON SCANNELL

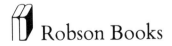

Robson Books

821
SCA

FIRST PUBLISHED IN GREAT BRITAIN IN 1975 BY ROBSON
BOOKS LTD., 28 POLAND STREET, LONDON W1V 3DB.
COPYRIGHT © 1975 VERNON SCANNELL.

ISBN 0 903895 58 7 Hardback
ISBN 0 903895 59 5 Paperback

Printed photolitho in Great Britain
by Ebenezer Baylis & Son Ltd., The Trinity Press,
Worcester, and London

Contents

For
James Corris

Acknowledgements

Acknowledgements are due to the editors of the following journals in which a number of these poems first appeared: *Cornhill Magazine, Encounter, The Listener, The London Magazine, Meridian, New Statesman* and *The Times Literary Supplement.*

The Loving Game

A quarter of a century ago
I hung the gloves up, knew I'd had enough
Of taking it and trying to dish it out,
Foxing them or slugging toe-to-toe;
Keen youngsters made the going a bit too rough;
The time had come to have my final bout.

I didn't run to fat though, kept in shape,
And seriously took up the loving game,
Grew moony, sighed, and even tried to sing,
Looked pretty snappy in my forty-drape.
I lost more than I won, earned little fame,
Was hurt much worse than in the other ring.

Wicket Maiden

It is a game for gentle men;
Entirely wrong that man's spare rib
Should learn the mysteries of spin.

Women should not be allowed
To study subtleties of flight;
They should bowl underarm and wide.

Or, better still, not bowl at all,
Sit elegant in summer chairs,
Flatter the quiet with pale applause.

It shouldn't happen, yet it did:
She bowled a wicked heartbreak – one,
That's all. God help the next man in.

Enemy Agents

Expert in disguise and killing-blows,
Fluent in all languages required,
They wrote me ardent letters, but in code.
My vanity and ignorance combined
To make me perfect victim for their game.
I took them at face-value every time.

Repeatedly they practised their deceits
And I was fooled, but slowly I became
Alert and learnt few things are what they seem,
Few people, too; so I grew narrow-eyed
And wore suspicion's habit like a coat.
I boasted not just second but third sight.

But then the top man, whom I'd never seen,
The power above the throne as you might say,
Assigned a partner to me. I could see
At once that she was candour's self, her whole
Demeanour spoke of truth. I'll never learn.
Most ruthless of the lot, her cover blown.

Where Shall We Go?

Waiting for her in the usual bar
He finds she's late again.
Impatience frets at him,
But not the fearful, half-sweet pain he knew
So long ago.

That cherished perturbation is replaced
By styptic irritation
And, under that, a cold
Dark current of dejection moves
That this is so.

There was a time when all her failings were
Delights he marvelled at:
It seemed her clumsiness,
Forgetfulness and wild non-sequiturs
Could never grow

Wearisome, nor would he ever tire
Of doting on those small
Blemishes that proved
Her beauty as the blackbird's gloss affirms
The bridal snow.

The clock above the bar records her theft
Of time he cannot spare;
Then suddenly she's here.
He stands to welcome and accuse her with
A grey 'Hello'.

And sees, for one sly instant, in her eyes
His own aggrieved dislike
Wince back at him before
Her smile draws blinds. 'Sorry I'm late' she says.
'Where shall we go?'

Separation

They stand still as trees
In the drifting mist
Of an autumn evening,
Silent as elms
With branches becalmed,
All language drowned,
A man and a woman
Quite motionless,
Yet the space in between
Is slowly increasing.
No gesture from either,
Regret or farewell,
As the interval widens
And they wait for the night
In stillness and silence,
For the moon's blind stare
Or the seal of darkness.

An Anniversary

Endlessly the stream slides past,
Jellies each white flat stone
Which stares through its slithering window at
The sky's smeared monotone.

Two willow leaves glide smoothly on
The water's shimmering skin;
Inches apart they float along,
The distance never changing.

Once, on a branch in the sun, they danced
And often touched each other;
They will not touch each other again,
Not now, not ever.

Marriage Counsel

Your problem is not unusual,
Indeed its absence would be that
(Regard this room as a confessional,
Nothing you tell me will leak out).
So far, it seems, your principal trouble
Is your wife's indifference, her failure to hear
Whenever you speak, in bed or at table,
Her remote and unrecording stare.
These are not uncommon features of a marriage,
In fact the contrary would be true.
You suspect an urgent need for copulation
With an unknown someone, the opposite of you?
She puts black stuff round her eyes and wears
Unaccustomed underclothes,
Ambiguous, weightless as mist? She dyes
The grey bits of her hair and shows
A strange new taste for vulgar romantic songs?
None of this need suggest another man.
You say she has never had strong lungs
Yet, despite Government Health Warnings, she has begun
To smoke cigarettes – expensive, King-size.
It may be the menopause, although
Her new vocabulary might give cause
For perturbation. It could show
That she is being refashioned utterly,
Which certainly suggests a mentor, a new friend.
In this case you must try to be
A different person too. It need not be the end.
Re-woo her. Win her hand again.
And if you fail – which might well occur –
This reflection should ease the ensuing pain:

Consider – you will not really have lost her
Because, from all you say, she is other
Than the woman you married. She is remade.
In this case you have never possessed her
And cannot therefore be betrayed.
Later, the former, the familiar wife
May return. It has often happened before.
But, if she does, do not expect life
To be suddenly charged with honeyed splendour
And harmonious chords. You must not be surprised
If you find your need and passion are dead.
There are times when defeat is to be prized
Above victory.
    Good day to you. You will forget
All I have said.

When Love Has Gone

When love has gone
This at least, or most, stays on:
When tenderness
Fades and brittles till the press
Of days destroys,
All arias are pulped to noise,
Prismatic dome
Drained and stunned, cold monochrome,
This need remains:
To clamp each other in soft chains,
The dragging links
Of flesh and, as the last flame sinks,
In darkness drown
Clinging, bearing each other down.
And yet, God knows,
You could not tell these cries from those
That used to flow
When love, it seemed, would never go.

Captain Scuttle Ashore

I've sailed so far and heard the sea's
Drunk shanties rolling under
A moon as fat and powder white
As a spot-lit prima donna.

Black sea ran through my hempen veins;
I drank it down like porter;
My heart was calloused like my hands,
I pissed and bled salt water.

But I'd one pretty whistle in my ditty-box
And, man, the tunes it's played
In knocking-shops and snazzy flats
From Brest to Adelaide.

In shacks and pads and pent-houses
And on the sun-burnt sands,
And once in a Methodist chapel,
I laid them all, like plans.

But this soft inland breeze that sighs
Now I'm ashore for good,
Brings a warm sweet rain that pierces me
As never north sleet could.

And my old concertina heart
Is squeezed by cunning fingers;
No jig or hornpipe rollicks out
But a melody that lingers,

A melancholy air that floats
Through twilight of the blood
And curls around the nervous roots,
Yet is not wholly sad.

There's a kind of joy in the tune that leads
Me to this breathing shore
Where, warm in the briny undergrowth,
I know I'll sail no more.

I'm home at last, I'm harboured now,
Tied up till the day I die,
Held fast by ropes of glossy hair
And anchored to a thigh.

Though white ships round my blue skull glide
And storms bang far and deep,
I'll stay where the waves like lions prowl in
And, tamed, lie down to sleep.

I Love Her Face

I love her face
because it is a statement,
unwasteful and complete,
of what she is.
Her eyes, kind knives,
shrewdly interrogate
the metaphysical heart
that lies within
this functional pump.
Her mouth, her nose, her ears,
their singular conjunction,
humble me.
Vocables kneel down,
mute celebrants.
Then this conjecture strikes,
cold-knuckled, cruel —
if, by some sudden accident
or gradual assault
of larcenous years,
her face were marred,
irremediably scarred,
eyes' brilliance doused,
would love then be reduced,
broken, dispersed?
Oh no,
for I would see,
beneath the flimsy mask,
the dear original,
approve false imperfections
that concealed
her beauty from untutored eyes,

and say, and say again,
simply, from the heart's own heart,
'I love her face,
her face is she.'

She Works at Tasks

She works at tasks
Requiring no especial skill,
Yet making their demands,
Hard to fulfill,
Demands on time and patience
And the capricious will.

Grease blears the gaze
Of water cooling in the bowl
And films her wrists and hands;
Toil takes its toll
Of strength, drains light and music
From the air and numbs the soul;

Or surely would
Except her love re-makes all things, '
And every trivial chore,
Transmuted, brings
A sacramental joy
And, while she works, she sings.

Amities

Amities composed in gentle weather,
Flowering in temperate field or harbouring wood,
Or sealed at ease in warm and fragrant bed

Flinch cravenly when winter swings its axe,
Raise hands in negative surrender when
Threatened by adversity's muscle-man.

It is the friendships built in bitter season,
When menace prowls the street and fields; when food
Is scarce and all you're left to share is need,

These are conjunctions nothing can unmake;
They will survive until all climates merge,
Proof against clock and calendar's furtive rage.

Spot-check at Fifty

I sit on a hard bench in the park;
The spendthrift sun throws down its gold.
The wind is strong but not too cold.
Daffodils shimmy, jerk and peck.

Two dogs like paper bags are blown
Fast and tumbling across the green;
Far off laborious lorries groan.
I am not lonely, though alone.

I feel quite well. A spot-check on
The body-work and chassis finds
There's not much wrong. No one minds
At fifty going the speed one can.

No gouty twinge in toe, all limbs
Obedient to such mild demands
I make. A hunger-pang reminds
I can indulge most gastric whims.

Ears savour sounds. My eyes can still
Relish this sky and that girl's legs;
My hound of love sits up and begs
For titbits time has failed to stale.

Fifty scored and still I'm in.
I raise my cap to dumb applause,
But as I wave I see, appalled,
The new fast bowler's wicked grin.

Self-Inflicted Wounds

Soldiers who decided that
dishonour was a wiser
choice than death, or worse, and spat
into the face of Kaiser
Bill and the Fatherland or
King George's Union Jack
and took up their rifles for
the purpose of getting back
to Blighty by sniping at
their own big toes or trigger-
fingers were called things like 'rat'
but preferred scorn to rigor-
mortis and considered gaol,
for however long, a soft
touch after trench and shell-hole,
but it is only the daft
who think that self-inflicted
injuries hurt less than those
sustained by folk addicted
to being punched on the nose
or greeting mutilation
welcomingly for the sake
of glory and the nation.
The wounds and scars that ache
the worst, and go on aching,
are from blows delivered by
oneself; there's no mistaking
that sly pain, and, if you cry,

you cannot expect a breath
of sympathy; you will find
no healing of any kind
till he comes who began it
all, and cures all, Doctor Death.

The Wrong of Spring

Oh, this risen beauty, treacherous and cold,
Concealing in yellow sleeves its glittering knives
Intended for the tender parts of coves
Who are too old
To dance on green a lithe white measure now,
It is unbearable — well, almost so.

And we grey inconsolables remain
Immured in winter's club; each holds his card
Of membership for which he's overpaid,
And through the window
See daffodils and girls, recalling how
We too walked golden there so long ago.

We dare not venture out; the knives are sharp;
The wind, the flowers, those limbs so delicate,
Yes, even they can pierce the faltering heart;
And we are prudent men
Not warmed by dreams of our lost Aprils, nor
By how we longed to be club-members then.

Our Father

'I was surprised,' my old friend said one night
As we sat there with our drinks and talked
Companionably of things
Linked by threads as thin as our grey hairs,
'I was surpised to find, when I was quite
Grown up – ready to try my wings –
Not that I hated Dad,
But there were many lads who claimed that they loved theirs.

'My father really thought that he was God
And sat upon his own right hand –
So that it couldn't see
What tricks the left was up to: sinister
Was just the word for what that member did.
He seriously claimed to be
Pure beyond reproach:
Pure hell the punishments he would administer.

'A sadist, liar and a fornicator
And, worst of all, strict temperance man,
The perfect hypocrite.
Not once do I recall a single word
Of kindness or affection from dear pater:
He was, in short, a total shit.
I never saw him smile
Far less laugh out; oh yes, he was a walking turd.

'Perhaps you think that I exaggerate,
Oedipal loathing has upset
My power to see the man?
Not so: I saw him on his dying bed.
I feel for him more pity now than hate;
I wish him peace. He lay in sweat
And silence for nine days,
Then spoke. "I'm sorry!" were the last words that he said.'

Wish You Were Here

The sun's brass shout is muffled by a wad
Of woolly cloud; this wind has wandered from
An earlier mood, say March.
Its energy has no good humour in it.
It floats a shiftier beach a foot above
The firm original,
Insinuates grit in sandwiches and eyes.

In spite of drifting sand, a muted sun,
We all, in our own ways, apply ourselves
To this, our annual task
Of relaxation or more active pleasure.
A yellow plastic ball bobs out to sea;
Young men with muscles prance
Or pose and touch their bulges pensively.

They do not touch my heart, as children do
Whose serious play is wholly lacking that
Self-consciousness that robs
The body's speech of plausibility.
The children ply their spades with diligence
Or dare the slavering waves.
Unknowingly they mould a memory.

The old are unselfconscious too. The wives
Lie back in deck-chairs, eyes tight-shut against
The wicked wind-blown sand.
Their husbands, bald and bracered, sleep until
The pubs renew their welcome, opening
Their doors like loving arms.
Incontinent and feline seagulls yaup.

And I, who feel I'm neither young nor old
But obsolete, lie on my bed of beach
And feel the sabulous wind
Spreading its thin coarse sheeting over me.
Ambition, hope, desire are cold. I'll stay
For sand to cover me,
Forgotten culture, not worth digging for.

A Circle of Animals and Children

The first animals spoke in the darkness,
Comforting. They uttered very simple words.
Their fur was familiar and their names
Easy to say. They had small eyes that never blinked.

I loved them, if love is being grateful
For their presence in my bed. This could be so.
They never disobeyed and seldom hid –
Teddy, Bunny and Jumbo with hide of velvet.

Next came the animals who could not speak:
The hamster, rabbits and cocker-spaniel
That looked like a black compassionate judge
Who would sentence no one. I loved him and liked most dogs.

Until my first child was born. This changed things.
All my delighted tenderness, fear and joy
Were concentrated through a burning-glass
Of gratitude and awe. I had no love to spare.

I watched my son, saw him learning to love,
The first and fumbling rehearsal conducted
Among my old, almost forgotten pets
With chronically astonished eyes. He spoke with them.

And later, predictably, I saw him
Banish the animals who had shared his bed
And take to his heart a brisk terrier,
Giving the little yapper love for a season.

Until his first child was born. This changed things.
He left, with wife and baby, for New Zealand.
Later, my other children went away.
I was alone with time for animals again.

They are company through the winter evenings
By the fireside. They walk with me in summer.
I spoil them, solicit their tolerance,
My mongrel – black dog – and the animal of death.

Our Pale Daughters

When our pale daughters move in lamplight
Their long hair, black or golden, flows
And waterfalls on shoulders, eyes

Contemplate a time and place
That never was nor will be, whose
Trees bear bells and dreams of veils.

But when our daughters move in daylight,
Their locks dammed up in scarves, they see
No trees or white lace in their street

But prams and dustbins, stubbled chins,
And hear cold choristers with lungs
Of steel singing of piston-rings.

Night Music

Darkness and the unceasing sigh and hush
Of the sea, sleepless below the bedroom window,
The slow and gentle molestation of the waves
Fretting the sand and pebbles, soothe the ear
Dismissing grit and sniggers of the day's
Vexations and perplexities, drowning
Those last invaders of the heart's repose.
   And then,
From the room beneath, the punctual music wakes:
Loved and loving hands walk thoughtful on the keys
As mother plays. Now sky and sea are wild
With bells and stars as bright arpeggios rise;
Silver scales – crunched moonlight – move in shoals
Beyond blind nets that reach into the dark.
The child swims through the window into sleep.

Those Childish Fears

Those childish fears
Would infuscate the brightest days,
Douse lamps, drain glitter from the sun's
Most scintillant rays,
Dam sleep with banks of poisonous talk,
Re-make your bed with sand and stones,
And freeze the dark.

And you believed:
The swallowed apple-pip could swell
Inside the belly, become a sick word
You could not spell;
The ambulance would come for you
To take you to a bandaged world;
It was all true.

One special fear:
Being carried off while wrapped in sleep,
Laid in the long box locked with prayers
And buried deep,
Then waking with black tons of earth
Pressing on lids and all your cries
Strangled at birth.

Then you grew tall,
Ate pips unharmed, did not go blind,
With logic swept old fears aside,
Spring-cleaned the mind.
Or so you thought. But now this season
Fades you find you are again afraid
And with good reason.

The Cowboy of the Western World

He rode into town one summer evening
As the bloodshot clouds presided over
The end of day, the leisurely pacing
Of decent citizens, most of them sober,
Though many intent on altering that.

He left his mount outside the saloon
And swaggered inside and called for liquor;
He felt that every eye in the room
Was fixed on his dangerous challenging figure;
He tilted the insolent brim of his hat.

His pants were tight and his heels were high,
Though his shirt was a temperate but sexy black.
He lit a cigarette, took another slug of rye,
Glanced round the joint then casually
Checked on his weapon with a nonchalant pat.

He stayed for an hour, but met no challenge.
Outside, the sky wore badges and spurs
Enough for a posse; a luminous orange
Spilt light on the sidewalk. When the shooting occurred
He was snug and dreaming in his bachelor flat.

Temptations

He is a christian gentleman
and very clean.
His wife is a christian gentlewoman
and at least as clean.
He speaks softly
and his smile is benevolent.
He is unfailingly courteous,
even to his wife.
You cannot imagine
either of them shouting.
And I sometimes wonder:
has he ever been tempted
to lash out, to go on a bender,
get pissed, smash glasses,
bawl bawdy in the street,
punch Proudpurse in the belly,
rummage under
Mrs. Grundy's skirts?
These reflections
are not intended
to censure or offend.
I am truly interested because
I have sometimes myself been tempted
to go on a jag of gentility,
to wallow in kindness and water,
to bow my wife through doorways,
speak softly and eliminate
all improper locutions.
Yes, I have been tempted,
not often and not for long,
but I doubt if I shall ever succumb.

Right Dress

Slither of silk like temperate water over
The humps of hips, delicious as a drink;
Lace froths on flesh as lightly as a shadow
And nylon shines, a sly translucent pink.

Next, the sheer stockings smoothing over knees,
Stretched taut at calves and plumping full of thighs.
The curtains at the bedroom windows press
Back, like constables, the straining eyes.

The sweet and private ritual of dressing,
This beautifying of the self, creates
A painless sense of being loved and loving,
A perfect equilibrium of states.

The frock floats like a fall of mist and roses
Over soft secrets, desiring and desired;
Before the wardrobe mirror gravely poses
Archibald Fullblood, Brigadier, retired.

All Things Come

Before the age of forty he was lithe
And reasonably handsome in his way.
Yet bullied by self-consciousness, he'd writhe
And mutter nothings if a woman lay
Too widely down or made a subtler pass;
And he was constantly distracted by
A shadow of a shadow in a glass.

He doubted everything, his strength, his looks
And gift, the praises of his friends and peers,
And even strangers who had liked his books;
He longed for lovely women but his fears
And vanity persuaded him to aim
Off target at the plain and dull whose ears
And eyes would fail to recognize his name.

At last he reached maturity to claim
Great honours and much public adulation
With decent dignity; and they came,
Whimpering and wild with adoration,
Women plump and fair or dark and thin,
Pleading for immediate consummation,
By which time rigor mortis had set in.

The Champions

A fanfare for these men, great in their way,
The dandy lad Jim Corbett and that huge
Jess Willard, Dempsey, Tunney, Grebb,
Heroes of an age of billycocks and jazz;
Siki, black as voodoo, swaggering through
Startled Harlem with a leopard on a leash,
Wilde, the frail assassin, and his friend,
Jim Driscoll, who could pulverize a man
Yet seem to be intent upon a strict
And lovely coreographic plan.
We should revere their brave
Refusal to be merely men,
Their dedication to a discipline
Whose end it is to demonstrate
That one can be more resolute and strong
Than seems the natural portion of our state,
Submitting to the limits of an art
As exigent as literature or love.
So I salute them all, the towering characters,
John Sullivan, Carpentier and Lynch,
No less because their majesty was worn
So brief a while before insulting time
Ripped it off and smashed the dazzling lamps
Above the ring and left them, small, alone,
In the dark and echoing hall of their defeat.

Lines to the Master

From more than thirty years ago, that first
Derisive summer of conscription, fear,
Young excitement, randiness and heat,
When, after sunset, widowed cities wore
Their weight of weeds, blind shrouds, black winding-sheets,
One memory endures, an obdurately bright
Taper in the dark loft of the skull,
The shape and sound of a quite unmartial event:
I saw a play performed. But more, much more,
I watched sheer mastery in action at its trade:
The sweet disease of love was charted with
A merciless and tender skill.
The play was *Romeo and Juliet.*
Since then astonished reverence for its maker
Has grown familiar yet no less powerful,
My homage wordless and involuntary
Until this stumbling dance of awkward praise.

I heard a music-hall comedian once
Chant a hoarse song, each quite unmemorable verse
Ending with this memorable refrain:
Shakespeare had a dirty mind.
Perhaps he had
If by this phrase we mean a mind that dug
Deep in the cledge and darker depths beneath,
Daring the dirt and worse, discovering gold,
Rare stones, gobbets and rags of rotten flesh,
Old bones, and deeper still the living roots
Of the multifoliate human tree.

I cannot think that he
Would much concern himself with theories
Equating poetry with less mundane arts.
I doubt if that most musical of poets
Would bow to Pater's axiom which implies
A dry imperative — all other arts
Aspire (or should aspire by implication)
To music's pure condition.

In middle age I hold few certainties
But here is one to last me to the grave:
He was, and is, the Master of them all.
He wrote our own and Everyman's biography
And at the last, alone in the sterile cave
On the desolate shore, his unrecorded cry
Would not have echoed battered Timon's roar.
He, who embodied all the savage truths,
Dissecting rage, ambition, lust and hate,
Possessed a serum that protected him
From his own creatures' worst contagions:
He was philanthropos and loved mankind.

The Poet's Tongue

With industry and patience he must bring
Together his great arsenal which stores
Blunt cudgels with the very latest thing,
Romantic swords employed in ancient wars
And complicated engines needing great
Skill and practice to manipulate.

And he must travel far in time and space,
Find loot in labs and factories, soil and sand,
Arrange his plunder in well-ordered ways
So what he needs will always be at hand.
And yet, possessing such elaborate means,
He'll constantly invite a puzzled stare
By using – not his intricate machines –
But bits of flint that hit the target square.

The Unknown War Poet

He enlisted among the very first,
Though not from patriotic motives, nor
To satisfy the spirit of adventure;
His was a different kind of thirst.
He believed incautious swigs of war's strong brew —
Orgasmic pain and terror, his own and others' —
To see Death's lavish make-up on the faces
Of the freshly taken would renew
The failing impulse to make globes of words,
Mysterious and lucid, passionate and cold;
And if he fell out of the sky or died
From bullet, blade or shellburst's sizzling shards,
His eloquence would march the earth he was;
Or, if the unrationed ocean swallowed him
Down in its deepest dark, the syllables
Would rise from submarine bone mouth like bubbles,
Endlessly amazing future eyes.
In fact he died before he wrote a line,
Blown to senseless pieces by a mine.
The poem of his body told no lies.

One That Got Away

I was alone, desultory line
Drifting in slow-pacing water
When suddenly I felt the tug,
Saw silver twitch in darkness shine
For no longer than a quarter
Of a second. Again, small jerk and drag

And momentary glitter: I knew I could
With skill and vigilance hook this one.
But then I was distracted by
Commotion on the bank where stood
Friendly idlers in the sun
Who, laughing, waved to catch my eye.

Politeness, or a slippier wish
To be esteemed, persuaded me
To greet them, swap some casual chat,
And then they left; but now my leash
Of line was slack; my prey slipped free.
I knew I could not win it back.

I wonder if another man
More serious, luckier than I,
Is richer for my careless loss,
As here in *The Angler's Rest* I stand,
Arms and tongue too short to try
To show how vast and marvellous it was.